Teachers' Devotions to Go

Helping You Focus on the Important Things

Diane Stark

D1569888

Copyright Diane Stark, 2019
All Rights Reserved

Published by Simple Joy

ISBN-13: 978-1-934626-38-2

Second Edition

Teachers' Devotions to Go

Diane Stark

A New Start

Now devote your heart and soul to seeking the Lord your God.

1 Chronicles 22:19 (NIV)

For most teachers, the start of a new school year is similar to New Year's Eve. We set goals for the year and promise ourselves that this year will be different than last year. We make "New School Year's Resolutions," and we do our best to keep them. Maybe, like me, your goals involve staying more organized and procrastinating less often. Maybe you'd like to see a change in a certain student or the way you teach a certain subject. Or maybe you'd simply like to be a better teacher than you were last year.

One resolution I make nearly every year is to worry less and pray more. And although I know this is something I need to work on in my life, I still find myself wringing my hands and chewing on my nails when all I need to do is talk with God about whatever is bothering me. I find that when

I set aside time for Him each day, I feel better and things go more smoothly.

And that's why I'm so glad that you've picked up this book. How wonderful that you've decided to start spending some time each day with God! Giving Him just a few minutes can make all the difference in how the day goes.

I've been where you are. Many, many times in my life, I've set the goal of having a daily devotional time with God. I've made that my New School Year's Resolution nearly every year of my teaching career because I know the difference it can make. But every single year, I've fallen short of my goal. I've gotten busy and missed a day. And one missed day turned into two, and then three. And then I just gave up. But a few years ago, I realized that I was totally missing the point of spending time with the Lord in the first place.

God doesn't want our daily devotion to be just another item on our lengthy To Do List. He doesn't want us to spend time with him because we have to; He wants us to do it because we want to. There's a reason that it's called a "devotion." According to Webster's dictionary, the word devotion means "profound dedication" or "an earnest attachment to a person or cause."

And that's exactly what God wants from us. He wants us to be "profoundly dedicated" to Him. Having a daily devotional time is just one way to show that dedication. When we love someone, we want to spend time with them. That's what God wants, simply to spend time with us. But He also doesn't want us to beat ourselves up when we miss a day. He doesn't want us to feel guilty. And He certainly doesn't want us to quit, or like me, just to try again next year.

Use your devotional time to show your dedication to God. Do as 1 Chronicles 22:19 says and devote your heart and soul to seeking God. The Bible promises us that when we seek God, we will find Him. (Matthew 7:7-8)

If you do miss a day, don't beat yourself up. And whatever you do, don't give up trying. It will make all the difference. In this life, and in the next.

Prayer: Lord, I know that You long to spend time with me each day. Please show me how important this time is and help me to make it a priority in my life. Amen.

A Little Time-Out

Enjoy a cup of tea while you do your devotion today. Make it a special time between you and God, a time you'll look forward to in the days to come.

Eyes on Me

Let us fix our eyes on Jesus, the author and perfecter of our faith, who for the joy set before him endured the cross, scorning its shame, and sat down at the right hand of the throne of God.
Hebrews 12:2 (NIV)

"One, two, three… eyes on me," I say to my kindergarten class when I want to get their attention. And just as I've taught them, they respond with, "One, two… eyes on you." And they all know that when they say those words, they'd better be looking at me, ready to hear the instructions I have to give them.

In my classroom, little tricks like that work as wonderful attention-getters. It's easy, doesn't take any planning or much time to do, and the kids enjoy it. They see it as a fun little game, rather than the classroom management tool it's designed to be. I've seen other teachers turn out the lights or clap their hands to gain their students' attention. I even knew one elementary school teacher who called out "Freeze!" whenever she wanted the floor.

These methods are usually surprisingly effective. My class would stop what they were doing as soon as they heard me say, "One." No matter how busy we were, or how noisy the classroom had gotten, I could still get their attention easily.

And all of this makes me wonder what methods God uses to gain our attention. In my own life, I know it's not always easy for God to get me to listen to Him. Sometimes I'm just too busy – and too stubborn – doing my own thing to worry much about what He might want me to be doing instead. But God has His own bag of tricks.

During a difficult time in my life, I spotted a bumper sticker that said "Keep Your Eyes on Jesus – He Always Knows the Way to Go." That simple sticker nearly brought me to tears and it was a wonderful reminder that no matter what was going on in my life, God was still there. That day, God used a bumper sticker to refocus my attention on Him.

God uses more traditional methods as well. He brings a Scripture to our minds at just the right time. He leads us to read a certain book or magazine article, or in this age of technology, the right email forward or website page.

Oftentimes, God puts someone in our paths to help draw our attention back on the Lord. He brings someone into our lives and uses that person to teach us what He needs us to learn.

And we all know that if you're going to learn anything, you've got to keep your eyes on the teacher. And as teachers, we need to keep our eyes on the Ultimate Teacher.

Prayer: Lord, help me today to keep my eyes focused on You. Help me to see what You want me to see and learn the lessons You'd have me learn. Amen.

A Little Time-Out

Today, use your eyes to only see the good things around you and use blinders against the negative. Focus on the positive aspects of your life, both at school and at home. You'll be amazed how your perspective will improve!

Right Beside Me

Be strong and courageous. Do not be afraid or terrified because of them, for the Lord your God goes with you; he will never leave you nor forsake you.
Deuteronomy 31:6 (NIV)

I had a big problem. My five-year-old daughter's baby-sitter had just called to say she was sick and couldn't take care of Julia that day. My husband had an important meeting at work, so he couldn't take the day off. And I was scheduled to take my class on a field trip to the apple orchard.

"Could you take Julia with you?" My husband suggested. "She's only a year younger than the kids in your class. She might actually have fun."

I called my principal at home to ask if today could become an emergency take-my-daughter-to-work-day. Thankfully, she said yes.

On the way to my school, Julia admitted that she was nervous about going on a field trip with the "big kids" in Mommy's class. She made me promise to stay right beside her all day.

When we arrived at the apple orchard, Julia clung to my hand – for about four minutes. Then some of the girls in my class invited Julia to ride on the tire swing with them. She grinned and ran off to play with the "big girls."

But a few minutes later, Julia looked around with a panicked where's-my-mommy expression on her face. She ran back to me and said, "Mommy, where did you go? I asked you to stay right beside me, but when I turned around, you weren't there."

I started to explain that she was the one who had run off, but she wouldn't listen. "Please stay by me, Mommy." And again, I agreed to do so.

The rest of the trip continued like this. Julia ran off with her new friends to chase a black-and-white puppy, to see a worm which had gotten stuck half-in and half-out of a green apple, and to kick the rotten apples that had fallen on the ground. But between each of these little adventures, she returned to me and scolded me for "leaving her."

While Julia's behavior seems silly to me, it reminds me of what I often do to the Lord. I get busy with my own life and put Him aside. But when something goes wrong and I need His guidance, I notice how very far away He seems. And I ask Him, "Where did You go? Why did You leave me?"

But God promises to never leave us nor forsake us. (Deuteronomy 31:6) So when He seems far away, I know that He wasn't the one to walk away. I was.

But the good news is that no matter how many puppies I chase or rotten apples I kick, God is always there, waiting for me to return to Him with open arms.

And He's waiting for you too.

Diane Stark

Prayer: Lord, thank You for Your promise never to leave me. Thank you for staying by my side through both the good and the bad. Show me what steps I need to take to have a closer relationship with You. Amen.

A Little Time-Out

Think about a few ways to improve the important relationships in your life. Then take a few moments to act on those ideas. Send an e-card to your spouse or child, write an encouraging note to a co-worker, or tell someone you're praying for them – and then actually do it.

(Teacher's) Lounge Lizards

Whatever is true, whatever is noble, whatever is right, whatever is pure, whatever is lovely, whatever is admirable – if anything is excellent or praiseworthy – think about such things.
Philippians 4:8 (NIV)

Many teachers use their lunch break to grade papers, fill out report cards, and do other teacher tasks. I see them in the teacher's lounge, eating their turkey sandwiches while frantically poring over a mound of papers. I truly admire their dedication, but I just can't do that. I have always felt that I was a better teacher in the afternoon if I allowed my lunch break to truly be a break.

So during my lunch time, I don't bring any work into the lounge. I eat and chat with the other non-paper-grading teachers. And, because I had some time to relax, I've always gone back to my classroom feeling refreshed and ready to take on the afternoon.

That is, until recently. Lately, after hanging out in the teacher's lounge, I've felt anxious and frustrated, and not at all rested. For days, I wondered what the difference was. And then I realized it was the topic of my conversations.

Many of them went something like this: "Last week I shared my lesson plans with Mary Jane, but this morning, I asked for her help and she said she was too busy. Can you believe her?"

And, "I can't stand the new policies the school district put into place. Those people don't know anything about actually being in a classroom."

Yes, it was sad but true. Many of my conversations were nothing more than gossip and complaints. The other teachers and I griped about nearly everything and then I wondered why I didn't feel relaxed as I headed back to my classroom! I was putting myself and others in a bad mood, simply because I was choosing to speak negatively.

In Philippians 4:8, the apostle Paul instructs us to think about only lovely, pure things. And obviously, this goes for what we talk about as well.

But when I think back to many of my conversations, I would hardly consider the things I said to be "noble" or "admirable." Often times, my words were negative, and sometimes, just plain rude. I knew I needed to make a change.

The next time you're hanging out in the teacher's lounge, pay close attention to your conversations. Are they in line with Philippians 4:8? Notice how much better you feel when your conversations remain upbeat. It's such a small change, but it can make a world of difference.

Kind of puts "focusing on the positive" in a whole new light!

Prayer: Lord, remind me to remain positive in my daily interactions with my students and colleagues. Help the words I say to glorify You.

A Little Time-Out

Make a list of 10 wonderful things about your classroom or school. Remember to look at this list when you need a pick-me-up!

The Paycheck that Really Matters

Whatever you do, work at it with all your heart, as working
for the Lord, not for men, since you know that you will
receive an inheritance from the Lord as a reward. It is the
Lord Christ you are serving.
Colossians 3:23-34 (NIV)

The day I signed my first-ever teacher's contract is a day I'll never forget. I was beyond thrilled to be doing something I loved as much as teaching, and to actually receive a paycheck for it was just icing on the cake.

Just minutes after signing my heaven-on-earth deal, I heard on the radio that NBA great Michael Jordan signed a contract to play basketball for the Chicago Bulls for one more season. The dollar figure in his contract made my teaching salary seem like just pennies. And truthfully, in comparison, it was.

Just moments earlier, I'd been on top of the world. But now, I felt deflated and underappreciated. I still recall complaining to my husband about the unfairness of it all. "Michael Jordan throws a ball into a hoop. I shape young lives," I griped. "How come he makes millions and I barely make five digits? It's just not fair. I'm making a real difference in the world."

Yes, it's true that teachers are grossly underpaid, while other less important professions receive the big paychecks. But we need to think of our salaries in terms of more than just money. We are rewarded with more smiles and hugs than most professions. We get more invites to graduation parties than anyone else. And there is the whole June, July, and August thing.

But more important than the benefits of teaching are the results of our work. We are doing far more than teaching children how to read and add. We are showing them God's love every day. Because of our patience, dedication, and service to our students, God's love is shining through us.

Colossians 3:23-24 says that we should work at everything we do as though we are working for God, and not for men. So if you are swamped with papers to grade, grade them as though you were doing it for the Lord Himself. And if you've fallen behind in your lesson plans, write them as though God was going to see them. Whatever work you do, do it in His name. When we work for the Lord, we will receive our inheritance from Him when we get to Heaven.

And I'd rather have that than Michael Jordan's paycheck any day.

Prayer: Lord, help me to remember that it's You I'm working for, not for my principal, the school district, or even my students. I work for You and that will have some wonderful benefits in due time. Please bless my efforts as I go about my day. Amen.

A Little Time-Out

OK, your paycheck isn't huge. But today, your assignment is to spend a little bit of it on something fun for yourself. Buy a romance novel, a new lipstick, anything chocolate, or best of all, another Devotions to Go book. Just enjoy it!

Diane Stark

I Have a Plan

For I know the plans I have for you," declares the Lord,
"plans to prosper you and not to harm you, plans to give
you hope and a future.
Jeremiah 29:11 (NIV)

Our beloved principal had resigned and the school district
had put a stranger in her place. This stranger's first order
of business was to "shake things up." Without even
meeting any of us, she assigned each and every teacher to a
new grade level. The week before the new school year
began, she sent a memo to the school saying that we
teachers had become "stagnant" by teaching the same grade
for years on end and she wanted us to "be professionally
challenged." At the bottom of the memo, the new principal
had written these words: "Trust me. I have a plan."

As you can well imagine, this change did not sit well with
many of the teachers. I had been a second grade teacher
the year before and the new principal assigned me to teach

kindergarten. I had some reservations about the change, but I knew I had gotten off easier than many of my peers.

"I don't think I can do it, Diane," said my dear friend Karen, close to tears. "I've been teaching first grade for 30 years and now some stranger tells me I have to teach fifth graders. I like little kids and I don't want to teach the older kids." She took a deep breath and said, "I'm going to resign."

My mouth dropped open. "Karen, you can't!" I protested. "You are a wonderful, amazing teacher and you'll be wonderful and amazing teaching fifth grade too!" I hugged her and added, "Plus I need you here."

Karen agreed to try. For the first few weeks of school, I could see the tension in her face as she adjusted to "the big kids." But by the end of September, she seemed to have come into her own. She laughed and teased her students, and she was obviously just as comfortable with them as she'd been with her first graders.

Toward the end of the year, the principal gave the teachers a choice. We could stay in our current grade level, or if there was a position available, we could move back to our old job. I chose to stay in kindergarten and was anxious to have Karen back across the hall in the primary wing. But she surprised me by choosing to continue teaching fifth grade.

She shrugged when she explained it to me. "I hated the idea at first. I couldn't understand why someone would force such a change on me. But the principal was right. She did have a plan, and she knew what was best for me, even when I didn't."

And in that moment, I was reminded that God also has a plan for us. Even when we don't understand it or when it isn't what we want in that moment, God is still in control and everything is going according to His plans. Although our plans don't always match His, we can read in His word that His plans for us will never harm us, but only bring us prosperity. In Jeremiah 29:11, He promises to give us hope and a wonderful future. God wants only the best for us, and He will give it to us, if we are willing to surrender our plans and follow His.

Prayer: Lord, I know that You are always in control and You have a wonderful, perfect plan for my life. Help me to put Your plan ahead of my own. Amen.

Diane Stark

A Little Time-Out

As you write out your weekly lesson plans, ask God for His help. Ask Him to show you where you could be more productive.

Life Long Learning

Let the wise listen and add to their learning,
And let the discerning get guidance.
Proverbs 1:5 (NIV)

"So, Diane, any big plans for the summer?" Asked a fellow teacher on the last day of school.

I sighed. "Oh, I wish. The only thing I've got going on is summer school."

"You're teaching summer school?"

"No, I'm going to summer school." I rolled my eyes and added, "My teaching license is about to expire so I've got six credit hours to take this summer so I can renew my license, and you know, keep my job."

She laughed and said, "I took my six hours last summer. And I have to be honest, it wasn't a lot of fun. I felt like I wasted my whole summer."

"That's what I'm worried about. But maybe it won't be that bad," I said.

She rolled her eyes. "Yeah, right."

The following week, I was back in the classroom, but as a student rather than a teacher. I wasn't exactly dreading the experience, but I definitely wasn't excited about it either. And in all honesty, my attitude wasn't the greatest.

In my own not-so-humble opinion, I was a rather competent teacher. I performed my job duties with both expertise and compassion. So, in that classroom that morning, my attitude was definitely one of "Why am I here? I already know everything I need to know."

As it turns out, I had a lot to learn, and I still do. In fact, the more I learn, the more I realize I need to learn.

The first class I took that summer was about encouraging slow and reluctant learners to succeed in the classroom.

The professor taught us to keep the stakes low when asking one of these students to take a risk.

In my kindergarten classroom, one of our favorite games is called "Beat the Teacher." It's as easy as can be, but the kids love it, year in and year out. Basically, I write whatever it is I want them to learn on index cards. In my classroom, it started with the letters of the alphabet and as the year went on, it progressed to sight words and easy-to-read words. Math facts work well too. The next part of the game takes a bit of acting – the more the better – and the kids love it. I look at the index card and waffle on about how hard this word is to read. I call on a student to "help" me and then show that child the card. If he is able to read it, I hand him the card. If not, I keep it. If the student gets the card, his classmates cheer. If he misses it and I keep it, the rest of the class will usually groan. At the end of the game, if the class has more cards than I do, then they "beat" the teacher.

I say the kids love this game, but I always have one or two students each year who really dislike being put on the spot.

Some students just get really nervous if they are called on. Once I learned that about certain students, I would just purposely call on them for an easy word. I assumed that the child was worried he would miss the word and that was the reason behind the nervousness.

Because I have not a single shy bone in my body, it never occurred to me that some people don't like to have the spotlight on them. I never realized that for some people, being the center of attention is an uncomfortable feeling, no matter how capable they are at the required task.

So in my summer classes, I learned something about sensitivity. My little "Beat the Teacher" game is hardly a low stakes proposition for a six-year-old. If a child misses a word, the whole class will know. And that's stressful for a kid. And I never even thought about it that way.

So I've altered the game to make it much less stressful for a reluctant learner or a quieter student. Now, each child has a wipe-off board. I say the word, they write it down, and hold up their boards. I take a quick peek and estimate how many kids got it right. That's how many points they get, and I get the points for the kids who misspelled the word. No one knows who was right and who was wrong. And now, when I say the kids love the game, I mean, all of them love it.

This was a lesson I learned, even when I thought I already knew everything I needed to know. But in Proverbs 1:5, it says, "Let the wise listen and add to their learning, and let the discerning get guidance." What that means to me is that one can never be too wise. And that the truly wise are always seeking to learn more.

This doesn't mean that I'll look forward to my next round of summer classes, but I will go into it with a much better attitude.

Diane Stark

Prayer: Lord, help me to realize that teaching – and life, in general – requires life-long learning. Help me to be humble enough to seek guidance when I need it and to get it from the best possible source, and that's You, Lord. Amen.

A Little Time-Out

Today learn something new about a topic you enjoy. It can be a beauty secret, a time-saver for your home or your classroom, or even a bit of useless information that brings a smile to your face. Whatever it is, just use it to remind yourself to keep on learning.

Diane Stark

The Big Oops

Forget the former things; Do not dwell on the past.
Isaiah 43:18 (NIV)

It was the week before Valentine's Day and I was preparing my weekly newsletter that went home with my students. I needed to include a class list so that the children could address their Valentine cards to one another. I was running late, so I used "cut and paste" to transfer my class list onto the back of the newsletter. I printed it and sent it home with every student without giving it another thought.

The morning of our Valentine's Day party, one of the little boys in my class said, "Mrs. Stark, you left Abby's name off of the Valentine card list."

"Oh, I couldn't have, Honey. Let me see." But to my horror, Stephen was right. I had carelessly used a class list from the beginning of the school year, so the child that had transferred halfway through the year was not on the list.

"Oh, no," I said. "How could I have done this?"

"It's OK, Mrs. Stark. Abby won't be left out," Stephen said. He opened his backpack and held it up for me to see. It was overflowing with Valentine cards, and most of them had Abby's name written on them. "My mom and I realized your mistake last night, so we took all of my extra cards and wrote her name on them." He smiled and added, "So she won't feel bad at all."

"Oh, Stephen, thank you so much! That was so thoughtful of you," I gushed.

And when his mother came in a few minutes later, I thanked her too. "It just breaks my heart that poor Abby would have been left out because of my mistake. I should have been more careful."

Stephen's mom patted my back. "We all make mistakes, so don't be so hard on yourself."

"Yes, but this particular mistake was a biggie. It could have resulted in a little girl being completely left out on Valentine's Day." I shook my head, still embarrassed that I had been so careless.

It was then that Abby smiled at me and said, "Mrs. Stark, did you see how many Valentine cards I got? I think I have more than anyone else!"

Stephen's mom smiled. "I think you can let it go now."

Like many people, I have a tendency to be my own worst critic. I am much harder on myself than I would be on anyone else. I have trouble forgiving and forgetting my own errors, but I will overlook them in other people. While this characteristic can be helpful in some ways, most of the time, it's not a good thing.

God doesn't want us to beat ourselves up for our mistakes. He forgives us and He wants us to forgive ourselves. As Isaiah 43:18 says, "Forget the former things, do not dwell on the past."

Living in the past and dwelling on the "shoulda, woulda couldas" doesn't help anyone. Besides, if the God of the Universe can forgive us, shouldn't we forgive ourselves?

Prayer: Lord, thank You for Your amazing forgiveness and grace. Help me to extend that same forgiveness to myself when I mess up. Amen.

A Little Time-Out

Is there something from the past you are still dwelling on? If so, it's time to let it go. Ask God for forgiveness and then forgive yourself.

The Best Laid Plans

Forgetting what is behind and straining toward what is ahead, I press on toward the goal to win the prize for which God has called me heavenward in Christ Jesus.
Philippians 3:13-14 (NIV)

"Today's the big day, huh?" The teacher across the hall said with a smile.

"Well, everything is ready," I said. "I've gone over it and over it. It should go smoothly."

"It" was my very first evaluation as a teacher. The principal was scheduled to come into my classroom and watch me teach for 30 minutes. She would then write an evaluation which would go into my permanent file. I had planned for a perfect lesson, including bribing my class with lollipops if they behaved while she was there, but I was still nervous.

The lesson I was teaching that day was based on the Dr. Seuss book, "Ten Apples Up on Top." I was going to read the book aloud to the class, we were going to pick out some of the rhyming words, and then I had a craft project for them to do based on the book. For this project, I had purchased several packages of fuzzy pom-poms and carefully pulled out all of the apple-colored ones. (That would be the red, yellow, and green ones.) I even remembered to get glue bottles, rather than glue sticks, because they stick better with the pom-poms.

The kids were to draw a picture of themselves, then glue some of these pom-pom 'apples' on top of their heads, just like in the story. They were then to write a sentence telling how many apples were on their head. I know it sounds simple, but for brand-new kindergartners, this was an ambitious undertaking.

Everything went smoothly while I was reading the book and discussing the rhymes in it. Every child was quiet and attentive. (They must have been thinking about their lollipops.) I sent the students back to their tables and handed out the pom-poms and the brand-new glue bottles. It was just moments later when complete chaos broke out.

"Mrs. Stark, my glue won't come out!" Multiply that times 22 five-year-olds.

All with the principal watching.

I grabbed a glue bottle and began to squeeze the tip, hoping to get the glue to come out. Nothing worked. Finally, I took the cap off and saw that there was a safety seal that had to be removed before the bottle would work. And of course, it was a child-proof safety seal.

So, again with the principal watching, I ran around to 22 five-year-olds trying to remove these seals. The principal even took pity on me and removed a few herself.

And when it was over, I knew I was sunk. I was convinced that the non-working glue bottles would be a huge blight on my evaluation. I even worried that the terrible evaluation would keep my contract from being renewed. And I beat myself up for failing to plan out that tiny detail of the lesson.

But I was silly to worry. When I got the evaluation back, it didn't even mention the faulty bottles. When I asked my all-too-kind principal about it, she shrugged and said, "That stuff is going to happen when you work with little kids. It's not whether it happens or not. It's how you deal with it that matters. And you dealt with it and moved on. As long as you get past it, it's no big deal."

I've always remembered my first teaching evaluation and that principal's kind words. We're going to make mistakes, in our classrooms and in life. It's how we deal with the situation that matters. So when you goof up, do what the apostle Paul says in Philippians 3:13-14. Forget what is behind you – you can't change it anyway – and move forward, doing the best you can in the future.

Prayer: Lord, help me to remember that I'm going to make mistakes. Help me to move past them and forget about them, so I can do my very best for You, Lord. Amen.

Diane Stark

A Little Time-Out

Exchange a humorous "I goofed" story with a fellow teacher. And if you don't have one, just tell her one of mine. (I have plenty!) It'll give you both a good chuckle.

Welcome Back

But while he was still a long way off, his father saw him
and was filled with compassion for him; he ran to his son,
threw his arms around him and kissed him.
Luke 15:20 (NIV)

"Bye, Tessa, we'll miss you," I said as I squeezed the little girl in my arms. Tessa had only been in my classroom for a few months, but I had gotten quite attached to her. She had come to our school right before Christmas and now, in March, she was leaving again. The reason for this was even harder to accept: Tessa was a foster child. She had been removed from her biological family and placed in foster care. But now, the courts had decided that she should return to her biological parents. And they lived in a different school district.

It was hard to let her go, not knowing what she would face when she went home. But the little girl was happy to be returning to her mother, so I was happy for her.

A few weeks went by and all of my students seemed to adjust to Tessa's absence. Except for one little girl. Vickie asked me every single day when Tessa was going to come back to our school.

"I don't think she is, Honey," I said. "I know you miss her, but she's going to a different school now."

Vickie's eyes filled with tears. "But she's my friend."

"I know, but she's happy where she is now," I said, not realizing how wrong I was.

Over the weekend, Tessa's foster mom called me at home. "The case worker just brought Tessa and her brother back to me," she explained. "I don't have all the details, but something happened." Her voice broke as she added, "She looks awful. She's covered with bruises."

I was both heart-broken and angry. The foster mother and I decided that it would be best to keep Tessa home from school until the bruises faded, probably about a week.

"The kids will be so happy she's coming back," I said.

At school on Monday, I told my class that Tessa would be returning to our class. They were thrilled and immediately, they wanted to make cards and signs to welcome her back. The kids' projects turned out beautifully and I looked forward to the following Monday when Tessa would be coming back to school.

But when her foster mother brought her in the next week, Tessa didn't want to come into the classroom. "I don't want my friends to see the bruises," she said. "Can't I just stay home a little longer?" She begged her foster mom.

I started to explain that her friends missed her and just wanted to see her again, no matter what she looked like. But something interrupted me. It was little Vickie. She'd recognized Tessa's mom's van in the parking lot and was sprinting down the hall toward her friend.

"Tessa! You're back! You're back!" Vickie screamed. "I missed you so much!"

Tessa opened her arms and the two girls hugged for a long time.

When they finally parted, Tessa smiled and said, "I'll stay."

And not one child in my class even mentioned Tessa's bruises. They were so happy to have their friend back, it was like they couldn't even see them.

This story reminds me of the parable of the Prodigal Son in Luke 15:20. A son leaves his family and squanders his inheritance. When he runs out of money, he decides to go home and see if his father will hire him as a servant. But his father had been waiting for him to return home and he welcomes him with love and forgiveness.

The parable is, of course, an analogy of God's great love toward us. No matter how far we stray, He is still anxiously waiting for us to return to Him. Nothing we could do is too bad for God to forgive us. His love for us is that strong.

Prayer: Lord, thank You for your love and forgiveness. Thank You for loving me, despite my mistakes and shortfalls. Help me to love and forgive others for their mistakes as well. Amen.

A Little Time-Out

Have you been a Prodigal Son (or Daughter?) Maybe not in your faith, but in another area. I am a Prodigal Scrapbooker. My acid-free paper and photo cropper have been waiting for me for far too long. So this week, I am going to find some time to get back to my favorite hobby. And you should too!

Playing Favorites

For the Lord is good and His love endures forever;
His faithfulness continues through all generations.
Psalm 100:5 (NIV)

On the playground, I overheard two little girls from my kindergarten classroom arguing over which child in the class was my favorite.

"I think it's me," said one of them. "I always know the answer when Mrs. Stark calls on me and I don't talk when I'm not supposed to."

The other little girl insisted that she was my favorite student. "I think she likes me best. Remember the time when I brought cheese crackers for snack and Mrs. Stark said they were her very favorite?"

The girls argued for a few more minutes before coming to me to solve their disagreement. "Which of us is your favorite?" They wanted to know.

I smiled and said, "I like every child in our class. I really don't have a favorite."

But the girls weren't buying it. "You have to like us better than some of the others," they said. "Especially the boys," they added in a mock whisper.

I laughed. Several of the boys had gotten in trouble for playing in the restroom that morning, and the entire class knew I hadn't been pleased with their behavior. "Just because I don't like something a child did doesn't mean I don't like that child," I said.

"I know you don't like Chad," one of the girls insisted. "He doesn't even know all of his letters yet."

"And Bradley is always playing with his scissors when he's supposed to be paying attention," the other pointed out. "We know you don't like him."

I again insisted that I did like every child in my class. The girls sighed, finally understanding that I wasn't going to admit to having a favorite student, and they ran off to play.

As I sat and watched my class play, I reflected on the girls' words. Did I really have a favorite student? Some children were certainly more cooperative than others. Some learned more quickly than others and some were even cuter than the rest.

So did I have a favorite? I guess, maybe, I did have a few students whom I was especially fond of. I think it's human nature to enjoy the children who always behave and learn quickly, and basically make my job easier, just a little bit more than the more challenging students. I'd love to say that I liked each child exactly the same, simply because they were in my class, but it wouldn't be entirely true.

But sitting on that bench, I realized that God loves each of us exactly the same, simply because we are His children. He doesn't love us because we attend church every single Sunday or because we try to keep the Ten Commandments.

He doesn't label us "good" or "bad." He loves each and every one of us as though we were His only child. In a word, we're all His favorite.

God's love isn't performance based. We don't need to earn it and we can't ever lose it. It's a gift he offers every one of us and all we have to do is accept it. The words, "His love endures forever" appear in the Bible more than 40 times. If God said He loves us that often, He must really mean it.

Being in God's class sure has some benefits, doesn't it?

Prayer: Dear Lord, thank You for loving me, even though I don't deserve it. Please help me to show love to the children I teach, especially when they don't deserve it. Amen.

A Little Time-Out

Tell someone special how much you love them. Better still, tell them how much God loves them.

Diane Stark

Under Control

Trust in the Lord with all your heart and lean not on your
own understanding;
In all your ways acknowledge him, and he will make your
paths straight.
Proverbs 3:5-6 (NIV)

"When I found out that Connor had you for a teacher, I was disappointed," one mom told me at our parent teacher conference.

Ouch, I thought to myself, but kept the look on my face neutral.

"Oh, it was nothing against you," she added quickly. "It's just that Connor's older brother had Miss Thompson and I kind of wanted Connor to have her too."

I shrugged and said, "You could have requested that he be placed in her class."

But she smiled and shook her head. "I thought about doing that, but something told me not to. And now I'm really glad I didn't. Because I see now that Connor got the right teacher for him."

Connor's mom went on to explain that while Miss Thompson and I are both wonderful teachers, we have very different styles. Miss Thompson does not yet have kids of her own and her expectations of her students are very high. Expectations that Connor's brother was ready to meet. Connor's mom said I am more of a "Mommy-Teacher." (I think she meant it in a good way!) Connor was less mature and school-ready than his brother, and he needed a little bit more patience and coaxing to meet his potential. And apparently, my teaching style was just right for Connor's personality.

"I'm so glad I didn't request a certain teacher for Connor," his mom finished. "I'm glad I listened to that little voice in my head and just left things alone. It all worked out the way it was supposed to without my doing anything."

I smiled and nodded, grateful for this mom's approval and vote of confidence. But later, her words came back to me. A little voice told her to leave the situation alone and it still worked out the right way. How often had I worried about something and then taken matters into my own hands?

More times than I'd like to admit. When it comes to my worries, I tend to be an Indian giver. I give them to God and then I take them back.

And I do this over and over and over again. But Connor's mom's story reminded me that God has everything under control. We don't need to worry about things. We need to do what Proverbs 3:5 says: "Trust in the Lord with all your heart and lean not on your own understanding."

We don't understand a lot of things in this world. And I don't think we're supposed to. But we know the One who does understand, and when we put our trust in Him, everything will work out the way it's supposed to.

God has it all under control.

*Prayer: Father, thank You that You really do hold the world
– and all of our worries – in the palm of Your mighty hand.
No problem is too big – or too small – to give to You. Help
me to give it to You and leave it there. Amen.*

Diane Stark

A Little Time-Out

Today, instead of worrying over something, make an effort to pray about it instead. It's far more effective and you'll feel better too. If you're like me, and your "worry button" tends to be overactive, write today's verse on a Post-It note and put it where you'll see it often.

A Clean Slate

For I will forgive their wickedness and will remember their

sins no more.

Hebrews 8:12 (NIV)

My kindergarten students love writing on individual-sized dry erase boards and chalk boards. If you ask them to write their sight words or math problems on paper, they moan as though they're being tortured. But if you ask them to do the same task on a wipe-off board, they cheer. So most of the time, I take the path of least resistance and allow them to practice their skills the way they want to.

But a few years ago, I had a student named John who was not exactly trust-worthy with a dry erase board. No matter what I asked him to do, he would end up drawing pictures instead. He was quite talented and his pictures were always wonderful to look at, but he was nearly always off-task.

One day, the kids had out their wipe-off boards and they were supposed to be writing their sight words for extra practice. I walked around the room frequently to make sure everyone was doing as I asked. As I walked toward John's desk, I saw him frantically trying to erase what was on his board. But when I reached him, I saw that the picture was still there.

"Mrs. Stark, I'm sorry," he said. "I was drawing and I wasn't supposed to be. But now I can't get it off."

I reached for the marker in his hand. It was a permanent Sharpie marker, rather than a dry erase marker. "John, you were using the wrong kind of marker," I explained. "We have special markers for our wipe-off boards, remember?"

He nodded slowly and I could see he was trying hard not to cry. He'd been caught off-task – again – plus he'd ruined the wipe-off board by not following directions.

"John, I know you like to draw, but right now is not the time to do that," I said. "You didn't follow the rules and now you're going to have to make it right." 'Making things right' has always been a biggie in my classroom. If you break something, you fix it. If you make a mess, you clean it up. Sort of a punishment should fit the crime mentality.

"But, Mrs. Stark, I can't make it right this time," John said tearfully. "I broke your wipe-off board by using that marker."

"There's only one way to get permanent marker off of a dry erase board," I said. I grabbed a dry erase marker and drew over John's picture with it. When all of the permanent marker was covered with dry erase marker, I handed it back to John. "Try to wipe it off now."

John's eyes grew big as the whole mess came right up. In no time, his board was clean. "Wow, that was so cool," he said. "Can I do it again?"

"No, sir," I said firmly. "What you're going to do now is put away you dry erase board and get out some paper. Because you've got some sight words to practice."

"I have to use paper?" He began to complain and then realized that he was getting off relatively easy. He smiled a little and added, "Thank you for helping me clean off my wipe-off board."

This experience reminds me of the "clean slate" God offers each one of us. Like permanent marker on a dry erase board, there's only one way to remove the stain of our sin. Jesus died on the cross for that purpose, and if we accept His sacrifice, God will forgive our wickedness and remember our sins no more. (Hebrews 8:12)

And then, just like with John's wipe-off board, we are like a brand-new creation, clean and unblemished in God's eyes. What an amazing gift that is!

Prayer: Thank You, Lord, for the offer of a clean slate. Thank You that You allow us to start over when we fail and You don't hold those failures against us. Amen.

A Little Time-Out

Tell another teacher how to erase permanent marker from a dry erase board. (This really does work!) And then share how God will erase her sins and give her a clean slate too.

Creative Encouragement

Kind words are like honey –
Sweet to the soul and healthy for the body.
Proverbs 16:24 (NLT)

"Look, Mrs. Stark, I colored a picture for you," said James, a sweetie in my kindergarten class.

I smiled my biggest smile and took the paper from him. "Good job," I said. "I'm going to hang it on the bulletin board behind my desk."

The boy beamed and went back to his seat.

The next day, James brought his math workbook for me to check. "All of your sums are correct," I said. "Good job!"

James smiled and went back to his seat.

But the following day, when I praised James with the words, "Good job," he frowned and said, "Why do you always say that?"

Caught off guard, I said, "Because I want you to know you did a good job and I'm proud of you."

"Then can you say 'I'm proud of you' instead? I don't like when you say 'good job' all the time."

I shook my head. "Honey, I'm not sure what you mean."

He sighed. "No matter what I do, all you ever say is 'good job.' You never say 'fantastic work' or 'way to go!'"

I thought back and realized that my young friend was right. Without realizing it, I did almost always praise my students using that one phrase. And after a decade in the classroom, he was the first child to point it out to me.

"James, I think you're right. I do say 'good job' too much, and I need to think of other ways to tell you that you are doing well in class. I'll try to work on that."

James smiled and said, "Thank you. Oh, and just so you know, I think you're a great teacher except for that one thing." He shrugged and added, "So keep up the good work!"

I laughed as the boy added, "See, Mrs. Stark, I didn't say 'good job!'"

Little James had made a valid point. I wasn't being creative in my encouragement, and it had lost its effectiveness. My students no longer felt good because of my words, even though they were meant to be encouraging. I had overused one phrase until my students barely heard it anymore.

Proverbs 16:24 says our kind words are like honey, sweet and healthy. When we sincerely praise our students' behavior, efforts, or attitude, our words encourage their souls and feed their spirits. So don't be like me and put your encouragement on auto-pilot. Think about what you say and make sure the words you use fit the students' actions.

Even if you don't realize it, they really are listening.

Prayer: Lord, please help me to use kind words with my students and other teachers today. Help what I say to reflect what's in my heart. Amen.

Diane Stark

A Little Time-Out

Do an internet search for "101 Ways to Praise a Child." This list will give you some new and creative honey-like words to use with your students.

Second Chances

He has removed our sins as far from us as the east is from
the west.
Psalm 103:12 (NLT)

"Robert, where is your math paper?" I asked.

The boy looked at me and shrugged. "I put it in the tray."

"Well, I don't have it." I got the other students' attention and asked them to see if they had accidentally taken Robert's math paper. No one had it so I began to look for it. Moments later, I found it in the trash can.

When I asked Robert why he put his math homework in the trash, he began to cry. "I'm sorry, Mrs. Stark," he said. "I don't know why I did it."

"This is very serious," I said. "Because not only did you try to skip doing your work, but when I asked you about it, you lied to me. Lying is not acceptable and I'm going to be speaking to your mother in the pick-up line today."

Robert cried harder and said, "Please don't tell my mom."

"Your mom needs to know about this because lying to adults is very, very serious."

When Robert's mother came to pick him up, I relayed the events of the day. She was quite upset that he'd lied and promised that she would talk with him at home.

But before he left, Robert threw his arms around my legs and sobbed. "Mrs. Stark, I'm so, so sorry," he said. "I'm really sorry and not just because I'm in trouble. I'm sorry that I did it. I'll never lie to you again."

I bent down and hugged him. "I forgive you, Robert, and I know you won't do it again."

Robert and his mother went home and I forgot about the incident. But the next morning, Robert brought me flowers from their garden and an apology note, written in his own handwriting.

"I'm sorry, Mrs. Stark," he said, getting teary-eyed once again. "I feel really bad about what I did."

"Robert, thank you for the flowers and the note, but you really didn't need to bring them. You said yesterday that you were sorry and I said that I forgave you. That's means it's over, Buddy."
"But I feel bad. I'm not a liar, Mrs. Stark."

I put my arms around him and hugged him. "I know you're not, and you need to stop worrying about this. You said you're sorry and that's all you can do. It's over."

"But do you still like me?"

I squeezed tighter. "Yes, of course, I do. You're a terrific little boy."

Robert sniffed and nodded slowly. I could tell it was hard for him to believe that it really was over, that I wasn't going to hold what happened against him.

And I think we often feel that way when we ask God for forgiveness. We remember our sins and keep track of them, but He doesn't. He forgets them completely when we ask Him to. It's like they never even happened. It says in Psalm 103:12, "He has removed our sins as far from us as the east is from the west."

There is an old adage that I really like. It says, "The man whose problems are all behind him is probably a school bus driver."

Your problems might not be behind you, but if you are a Christian, your sins are.

Prayer: Thank You for forgiving me, Lord, and help me to forgive those around me. Help me to truly "forgive and forget" when my students disobey. Amen.

A Little Time-Out

Today I want you to forgive yourself by taking some time off. Instead of grading papers, take a bubble bath. Instead of writing lesson plans, enjoy a cup of coffee or another treat. God loves you, so take time today to love yourself!

Diane Stark

Lessons in the Lay-Away

Rejoice and be glad, because great is your reward in heaven.

Matthew 5:12 (NIV)

Posted in my classroom is a giant cardboard stop light. My students know that too much talking and not enough listening will cause their name to be moved from the green circle to the yellow one. And if they misbehave again, their name will end up in the red section.

And that means a phone call to their parents.

Nick, one of my more challenging students, found his name in the red circle more often than not. Nick was not a bad child; he just struggled with self-control. If something looked like fun, he did it, regardless of the consequences.

Nick's mother and I had a wonderful relationship. She knew that he was acting up at school, and she and I were working together to reach a solution. Finally, one day, she

81

came to school and told me that Nick had chosen a bicycle, but instead of letting him have it, they'd put it in the lay-away of our local Toys R Us store. Nick's parents explained that if he made it through the school week without getting his name moved to the red circle of our stop light, they would put ten dollars toward the bike. And they wouldn't take the bicycle home until it was completely paid for. Even the store's manager was in on the plan, and he agreed to bend the lay-away rules so the bike could remain in the store indefinitely.

Nick's parents put the bike in the lay-away in October. And at first, we feared he'd never see it again. But gradually, Nick began to realize that his behavior had consequences. He wanted the bicycle, and he had to behave at school in order to get it.

It was a wonderful experience, seeing the changes in Nick. When I watched him, I could actually see him weighing the consequences of his choices. He began to think before he acted, and most of the time, he made the right choice. But life with Nick still had its ups and downs.

One time, Nick had stayed in the green or yellow circle every day that week, but on Friday, I caught him playing in the sink in the boys' restroom. (For some reason, school bathrooms seem to be where most of the mischief happens!) He was soaking wet, as was his partner-in-crime. And although I hated to do it, I moved both boys' names to the red circle.

"Please, Mrs. Stark," he said tearfully. "I've been good all week, but now that I'm on red today, I won't get my bike money for this week."

I shook my head. "I'm sorry, Bud. You should have thought of that before you made a mess in the bathroom."

Thankfully, Nick did eventually earn his bicycle. And that little guy earned a special place in my heart, as well. Of all the students I've ever had, he matured the most during his kindergarten year. He learned to make better choices because he was working toward a reward.

Matthew 5:12 says we have a great reward waiting for us in Heaven. But because of Jesus' sacrifice on the cross, we don't have to earn our reward through good works. We simply have to accept the incredible gift He's offered to us.

Prayer: Give me patience with my students today, Lord, especially the ones who try that patience the most. Help me to work with their families to reach solutions that will benefit all of us. Amen.

Diane Stark

A Little Time-Out

Sock away a few bucks from each paycheck (like your own little lay-away) and use it for something special. Maybe a massage or a manicure. Enjoy!

Inside Out Day

The Lord does not look at the things man looks at. Man looks at the outward appearance, but the Lord looks at the heart."
1 Samuel 16:7 (NIV)

Our school frequently has "Spirit Days," where the students pay a quarter to wear a specified item. Sometimes we have "Hat Day," or "School Colors Day." The money the kids bring goes to a charitable organization, like the Humane Society.

Recently our school sponsored an "Inside Out Day." The kids were supposed to wear their clothes inside out, and the more silly they were, the better. This special day was scheduled for Thursday, but on Wednesday, one of the little girls in my class came to school dressed for Inside Out Day. Her t-shirt and jeans were turned inside and her hair was pulled up into more than a dozen pony tails.

Samantha walked into the classroom, looked at me, and said, "Mrs. Stark, why didn't you dress for Inside Out Day?"

Before I could answer her, some of the other students entered the room. They pointed at Samantha's clothes and began to laugh. "Today wasn't the day to dress like that," they said. "You look funny!"

Samantha looked at me and said, "Why are they laughing at me? And why isn't anyone else dressed for Inside Out Day?"

"Inside Out Day is tomorrow, Honey," I explained. "Would you like to go into the bathroom and turn your clothes the right way?"

"I can switch my clothes, but I won't be able to fix my hair. My mom put hairspray in it, so if I take down the pony tails, it will still look crazy," she explained. Tears gathered in her eyes as she added, "But I brought a whole dollar to give. It's from my piggy bank."

"You are such a sweet girl," I assured her. "It's so thoughtful of you to bring money for the dogs and cats in the shelter. Thank you."

So Samantha went about her day, the only one with crazy hair and inside out clothes. A few of the other kids teased her, but I told them that Samantha had brought a dollar for the shelter, when the kids were only asked to bring a quarter.

"Samantha has a generous heart," I said.

"Yeah, but she has way too many pony tails in her hair," one of the little boy muttered.

The kids in my class were judging Samantha by her appearance. And even while I told them that their comments were not acceptable, I knew that I had been guilty of the same thing far too often. I have had students in the past who came to school unclean, and I judged them by their appearance. I have made judgments about people based on their clothing or even their hairstyle.

But we know that God doesn't look at those things. It says in 1 Samuel 16:7, "The Lord does not look at the things man looks at. Man looks at the outward appearance, but the Lord looks at the heart."

I don't always look at my students' hearts, but I should. I need to remember that it's the inside the counts, even on Inside Out Day.

Prayer: Lord, help me to see people the way You see them. Help me to see my students' hearts and not judge them by their outward appearances. Amen.

A Little Time-Out

Although outward appearances don't matter to the Lord, they do matter to us. When we look good, we feel good too. So take some time today to pamper yourself and improve your outward appearance. Buy a new outfit, a lipstick or a bottle of nail polish. Get a hair cut or a manicure. Do whatever makes you feel good!

Diane Stark

The Committee Crisis

But in fact God has arranged the parts in the body, every
one of them, just as he wanted them to be.
1 Corinthians 12:18 (NIV)

Every year, the teachers in my school have to choose what committee to join. Some committees are more fun than others and some require more work. Most years, almost everyone wants to be on the Social Committee. These are the people in charge of planning the Christmas party, celebrating staff members' birthdays, and recognizing the appropriate people on Secretary's Day, Teacher Appreciation Week, and Boss's Day. This committee is generally fun, but there is quite a bit of work involved.

There are a variety of not-so-fun committees and they usually have very few people volunteer for them. There is the Curriculum Development Committee, the Goal-Setting Committee, the Annual Yearly Progress Committee, the Standardized Testing Committee, and the list goes on and on and on.

One year, I missed the meeting where everyone signed up for the committee they wanted to join for that school year. So by the time the list got to me, there only one opening left. It was as the chairperson for the Standardized Testing Committee. I immediately felt frustrated that that would be my assigned role for the year. As a kindergarten teacher, my students do not participate in standardized testing, so I was clearly not the right person for this job.

I complained to several of my colleagues, hoping they would volunteer to trade places with me, but of course, no one did. Being the chairperson of any committee was not an enviable position in which to be, and the chairperson of this particular committee was simply the bottom of the barrel.

I pled my case to the principal, but she insisted that it would be "good for me" to "expand my horizons." I was not happy.

Over the course of that school year, I learned more about standardized testing than I ever wanted to know. I organized meeting after meeting and filled out tons of paperwork, all while envying my friends on the oh-so-easy Social Committee.

Toward the end of the year, I was complaining once again about my committee placement. One of my friends and fellow teachers was obviously tired of listening to me gripe. She said, "Hey, Diane, some one had to chair that committee. If it hadn't been you, it would have been one of us. Anyway, you did a really good job."

I rolled my eyes. "It's the worst committee ever."

She smiled and said, "Yes, but it's also one of the most important. And like I said, somebody had to do it. We all have a job to do, and this year, that job was yours."

I nodded, realizing what my friend was saying. It hadn't been fun, but it had been necessary. And it all reality, it had probably been my turn.

"You're right. I'm sorry I had such a poor attitude about it. I'll have to work on that. But do you think next year, maybe I could be on the Social Committee?"

My friend laughed and said she'd look into it.

Just like each one of us has a certain job to do in a school, we each have a job to do in God's family. Some of the jobs are glamorous, like singing a solo in front of the congregation. But most of the jobs that the Lord needs done are not so glamorous. Serving homeless people in soup kitchens, preparing the communion plates, and working in the church's nursery are all jobs that someone in God's family has to do. All of these things are behind the scenes, and there's not a lot of glory in them.

But someone has to do them and no job is more important than any other. 1 Corinthians 12:18 says, "But in fact God has arranged the parts in the body, every one of them, just as he wanted them to be." Just like in the human body, every one of us has a job and a responsibility in the Lord's kingdom.

Yes, some are more fun than others. But every job is important.

Prayer: Lord, help me to remember that You have designed a job especially for me. Help me to discover what that job is and to do it to the best of my ability. Amen.

A Little Time-Out

As teachers, most of us have realized that working with children is one of our God-given gifts. But we also have an incredible opportunity to nurture the gifts we see in our students. Today, make it a point to notice what the children around you are good at and try to encourage them in those areas.

Eyes in the Back of My Head

*Where can I go from your Spirit? Where can I flee from
your presence?
If I go up to the heavens, you are there; if I make my bed in
the depths, you are there.
If I rise on the wings of the dawn, if I settle on the far side
of the sea,
Even there your hand will guide me, your right hand will
hold me fast.
Psalm 139:7-10 (NIV)*

Many children believe that teachers – and mothers – have a super hero-like ability. The ability to see everything that happens around us, no matter how busy we are. Yes, I'm talking about the eyes we have in the back of our heads.

On numerous occasions, I have had students say, "Hey, how did you know I was about to pull Suzy's hair, or run in the hallway, or break one of our rules?" And I smile and say, "Teachers know everything."

I don't obviously, but with teaching experience comes a certain intuition that trouble is brewing. Sometimes, I can tell when one of my charges is thinking of doing something they shouldn't be, and I can head them off.

It happens on the playground quite often. We have a strict rule at our school that no one is allowed to run underneath the monkey bars. It doesn't matter if anyone is climbing on them at the time. I have seen too many children get kicked in the face, so we just made a blanket rule. The children just aren't supposed to run under the monkey bars. Period.

Of course, this doesn't stop them from being tempted. They seem to want to see how close they can get to getting kicked without actually getting a sneaker in the head. So when I'm on playground duty, I know to keep a close eye on the monkey bars.

One day while we were outside, I noticed that Connor was watching me intently. He would look at me and then glance at the monkey bars and then back at me. And I could see a plan hatching in his little mind.

I called him over to me and said, "Connor, you weren't going to run under the monkey bars, were you?"

His eyes grew big and he said, "How did you know?"

I just smiled and gave my trademark answer. "Teachers know everything."

Just then, one of the little girls went swinging across the monkey bars. She lost her grip and fell to the ground. She popped right up, unhurt, but Connor was stunned.

"Did you see that? Tara fell off the monkey bars and I was just getting ready to run under them. She would have fallen on me." His eyes grew even bigger and as he added, "You saved my life, Mrs. Stark."

I had to bite my lip to keep from laughing at Connor and his dramatic flair. I was just about to say that I doubted he would have sustained any life-threatening injuries from the monkey bar incident when he said something that really caught my attention.

"Wow, I see now why we have the rule about running underneath the monkey bars. Rules sometimes make things less fun, but they can also protect us from getting hurt."

And I realized how right Connor was. Our Heavenly Father makes rules that are not designed to make things less fun, but to protect us from harm. We make rules for our students because we care about their safety and well-being, and that's why the Lord gives us rules as well.

And just like my students feel like there is nowhere to go that I can't see what they're doing, the same is true with God. He always sees us and He always knows what we're doing. But this is meant to protect us, not to control us.

As today's verse says, wherever we go, we cannot flee from God's presence. No matter where we are, His hand will guide us and hold us fast. (Psalm 139:7-10) Even if we go to the far side of the sea, God loves us and wants only the best for us.

Even if we run underneath the monkey bars.

Prayer: Thank You, Lord, that You are always with us, no matter where we go, to protect us and guide us. Help me to follow the rules you've set out because I know they are there for my own protection. Amen.

A Little Time-Out

You might not be able to make it to the far side of the sea anytime soon, but you should still take a little vacation. Even if it's just an hour to enjoy a cup of tea and a favorite novel, take some time today just for you.

Diane Stark

One Way

Jesus answered, 'I am the way and the truth and the life.
No one comes to the Father except through me.
John 14:6 (NIV)

"Mrs. Stark, I don't feel well," moaned one of my students.

Just moments before, this child had been laughing and carrying on with his classmates. "Oh, I think you'll be all right," I said with just a touch of sympathy in my voice.

Not long after, another child came up to my desk. "Mrs. Stark, my head hurts."

I felt the child's forehead. "Well, you don't have a fever," I said, this time with more sympathy. "Put your head down on your desk for a few minutes and see if it feels any better."

And a few minutes later, yet another child came up to my desk with a complaint. (Feeling ill seems to be a contagious condition among the young children in my class.) Each child was sent back to their seat with a simple solution, such as "Oh, you'll feel better after you eat your snack" or "Just tell your mom when you get home."

That is, until Marissa stood up, holding her belly. "Mrs. Stark, I feel like I'm going to throw up!" She yelled. And I couldn't get her out of the classroom fast enough.

Even after all of my years around young children, I'm still not very good with vomit. I'm a squeamish person by nature and seeing someone else get sick just throws me over the edge.

It doesn't take my students very long to figure this out. If they tell me their head hurts, they get a hug and then sent back to their seats. But if they tell me they feel nauseous, they get a speedy-quick pass to the nurse's office.

The kids figure this out and they use it to their own advantage. There's only one way to get out of Mrs. Stark's class: Play the vomit card and you're outta there.

Over the course of a school year, I can usually determine which students are really feeling ill and who just wants to visit with our friendly school nurse when they should be doing math problems. But every once in a while, I guess wrong and somebody tosses their cookies in my classroom. It makes me feel bad for the child and it usually renews my automatic 'nausea equals you're-outta-here' policy.

My students know there's only one way out of our classroom during instructional time. And as Christians, we know there's only one way to get to Heaven. In John 14:6, Jesus says, "I am the way and the truth and the life. No one comes to the Father except through me." We can't be 'good enough' to get into Heaven. Nothing we can do will get us in.

There's one way and only one way. His name is Jesus and He made the way for us when He died on the cross for our sins. Jesus' sacrifice makes it possible for us to go to Heaven.

And He did it because He loves us more than anything.

Prayer: Heavenly Father, thank You for sending Your Son to die on the cross for my sins. Jesus took my punishment and He is the one and only way to be saved. Thank You for loving me that much. Amen.

Diane Stark

A Little Time-Out

There's only one way to Heaven, but there's lots of ways to relax. Make a list of your favorite ways to chill out and then choose one to do today. And choose one tomorrow too!

Because I'm the Teacher!

For my thoughts are not your thoughts,
Neither are your ways my ways,'" declares the Lord.
As the heavens are higher than the earth, so are my ways
higher than your ways
and my thoughts than your thoughts.
Isaiah 55:8-9 (NIV)

"But, Mrs. Stark, I don't know how to write yet," whined several of my kindergarten students.

"I know, Boys and Girls, I know," I said, trying to calm them down. A few of them looked ready to cry, which wasn't surprising, given the circumstances.

It was writing prompt day in my classroom and it was the first one of the school year. The administration required us to do four of them – one each grading period for the entire year. The purpose was to see how much they improved over the course of the year, not to see how well they could do after just a few weeks of kindergarten. I knew this, but no amount of explaining seemed to alleviate the stress for some of my students.

"OK, I need everyone to take a deep breath," I said in what I hoped was a soothing voice. "Listen carefully because I'm going to give the directions one more time. On the paper in front of you, I want you to write the words 'I like…' and then write or draw a picture of something you like." I smiled. "It's easy, right?"

Nope. It wasn't. "But I don't know how to spell 'like.'" Several of them protested. "Can't you write it on the board and we can copy it?"

"No, Boys and Girls, I can't do that this time. Again, it doesn't matter if you can't spell it just right. Just sound it out the best you can. And remember, this is just to see how we're writing in September. We're going to do this again a few months from now and see how much better we're able to do."

Still more protests and more tears. "But, Mrs. Stark, why won't you help me? I can't do this by myself."

And from one precocious child, "I don't understand why we're doing this. It doesn't make sense to me."

I answered, "That's why I'm the teacher and you're not. There are things that I'm going to ask you to do that you might not like. But you're going to do them anyway because I know what's best."

"But I don't understand," she continued.

"Just trust me. I know what's best," I said.

"But I don't know why we have to do this," she whined some more.

"Because I'm the teacher!" I finally said in frustration.

We somehow managed to get through our first writing prompt of the year, however painful it was for some of my students. But the next one in December wasn't so bad. And the one after that in March went better still. And by the time we got around to the final writing prompt in May, the kids were actually enjoying their writing time.

And when I brought out their efforts from the first month of school, they were astonished at the progress they'd made over the school year.

"Wow, look how well I can write now," they said.

"My goodness, I was such a baby then compared to now," they mused.

And I knew I had reached a teachable moment opportunity. "Boys and Girls, do you remember how long it took us to do our very first writing prompt? And how some of you almost cried because I wouldn't help you? Do you see now why I made you do it on your own? I wanted you to be able to see your progress at the end of the year."

The kids nodded, finally understanding that I had been right. That I had a good reason for what I was doing, and they wouldn't necessarily understand that reason because they were children. I was the teacher, and that meant that most of the time, I would know better than they did. And it was their job to trust me and do as I asked.

This story reminds me of today's verse. Isaiah 55:8-9 says, "'For my thoughts are not your thoughts, neither are your ways my ways,'" declares the Lord. "'As the heavens are higher than the earth, so are my ways higher than your ways and my thoughts than your thoughts.'"

God knows better than we do because He's God and we're not. Period.

We won't always understand the reasons why He does what He does. Or why He allows certain things to happen. But it's not our job to understand. It's our job to listen, and to trust, and to follow Him. And someday, we'll understand the reasons behind His actions. But until then, all that matters is this:

He knows what's best for us. And He loves us enough to give it to us.

Prayer: Thank You, Lord, that You truly do know what's best for me. Help me to remember that my ways are not Your ways, but my job is to trust You anyway. Amen.

A Little Time-Out

What are you going to ask God about when you get to Heaven? I know I've got a few questions for Him. There are things I don't understand, and I struggle to trust Him with these issues. Share one of your "I don't get it" things with your spouse, co-worker, or friend. It might make you feel better or give you both a good laugh. Either way, it's a blessing!

Too Many Rules

*The most important one is this: Love the Lord your God
with all your heart and with all your soul and with all your
mind and with all your strength. The second is this: Love
your neighbor as yourself. There is no commandment
greater than these.*
Mark 12:30-31 (NIV)

Every year on the first day of school, I ask my students to help me decide on our classroom rules. Without fail, most of the children's suggestions revolve around the prevention of physical and emotional pain.

This past year, when I asked my kindergartners what our rules should be, the first five suggestions I got were: Don't hit, don't kick, don't pinch, don't push, and don't pull hair. I nodded encouragingly, telling them these were all good ideas. And then I suggested that we combine all of those ideas into one big rule: Always keep your hands and your feet to yourself. The kids liked my suggestion.

I then asked them for other suggestions of rules for our classroom, and predictably, their ideas shifted from rules preventing physical pain to those preventing the emotional kind. Their suggestions now included: Don't call anybody stupid, don't say 'shut up,' don't tell anybody they can't be your friend, and even don't ever tell someone their Sponge Bob shirt is ugly. And once again, I suggested combining all of their very good ideas into just one rule: Always use kind words. And again, the kids thought that was a great solution.

I told my class that having just a few really important rules is better than having a whole bunch of little rules. Having just a few makes them easier to remember. And because there are only four or five, the kids seem to understand that all of them are important and must be obeyed.

And every year, as I make my rules with my new class, I am always reminded of the rules that God laid out for us. And no, I'm not talking about the Ten Commandments. I'm talking about the ones in Mark 12 where Jesus is asked which commandment in the most important. Jesus' answer is two-fold. He instructs us to love the Lord with all of our heart, mind, strength, and soul and to love our neighbor like ourselves.

He gave us just those two rules as "umbrella rules," – the most important ones – and all others fall under them. If you look at the Ten Commandments, you'll see that none of them can be broken without breaking one of the umbrella rules. You can't love God with all of your heart, but take His name in vain or worship something ahead of Him. And you certainly can't kill or steal from your neighbor if you are loving him like you love yourself.

So focus on God's main rules – loving Him and loving other people – and you'll always be doing the right thing.

Prayer: Lord, guide me as I patiently teach my students to follow rules. And remind me that Your most important rule is simply to love. Amen.

A Little Time-Out

Break the rules today! Instead of staying after school to grade papers, go home early and do something you enjoy.

Diane Stark

Rest Stop

Cast all your anxiety on Him because He cares for you.
1 Peter 5:7 (NIV)

Like most early elementary school teachers, I have always celebrated the 100th day of school with my students. We keep track of the days using straws or popsicle sticks. Every time we get another group of ten, we bundle them together with a rubber band. This helps the students learn place value, counting by tens, and other valuable math skills.

And when we get to the 100th day, we have a party. We make trail mix using 100 of each ingredient: 100 Cheerios, 100 M&M's, 100 raisins, 100 pretzel sticks, and 100 chocolate chips. It doesn't taste that great, but the kids love it. We make hats with giant 100's on them and eye glasses where the lenses are the zeroes. The kids bring in small items from home that must total 100. We do a variety of activities, all based on the number 100.

One year, on the 100th day of school, one of my students wished me a happy birthday. When I said, "Today isn't my birthday," he looked confused and asked, "Well, sure it is. That's why we're having this party. It's your 100th birthday, Mrs. Stark!"

But all joking and confused kindergartners aside, it's a really fun day and a milestone in the school year. But I also use it as kind of a "rest stop." In a 180-day school year, the 100th day is just over half-way. It's a day to rest, but also to analyze what is going well in your classroom and what things could be going better. It's a day to ask God to help you make the remainder of the school year a successful time for everyone.

Unfortunately sometimes, getting to that 100th day, and from there to the end of the year, can be a real struggle. A challenging student or work situation can make each day feel like an uphill battle. And that's why we need to lay each and every day at the Lord's feet. We need to ask Him for His help and His strength to do what needs to be done that day.

I Peter 5:7 says that we can cast our anxiety on God. Matthew 11:28 makes a similar promise. It reads, "Come to me, all you who are weary and burdened, and I will give you rest." God wants us to work hard, but He also wants us to rest and relax. He wants to carry our burdens for us.

Teaching is a wonderful, wonderful profession, but it's not an easy one. And that's why we're so lucky that we don't have to do it alone. Cast your worries on God. His shoulders are much bigger than yours.

Prayer: Lord, help me to remember to rest and take care of myself sometimes too. Help me to stop worrying and instead, give my burdens to You. Amen.

A Little Time-Out

It might sound silly, but today I want you to write a letter to God. Tell Him what you're thankful for. Tell Him what you're worried about. Tell Him what's on your heart. It'll make you feel better, I promise.

Chin Up!

I have told you these things, so that in me you may have
peace. In this world you will have trouble. But take heart!
I have overcome the world.
John16:33 (NIV)

I once had a principal who was not very supportive of her teaching staff. (And this, believe me, is putting it mildly.) She micromanaged us to the point that we thought we'd lose our minds. She had a long list of rules that we had to follow, and many of these rules seemed to rob us teachers of our ability to run our classrooms. And truthfully, many of us felt that she had robbed us of our dignity as well.

One of the most bothersome rules involved our hallway bulletin boards. The rule was that they had to be changed every Friday before we could leave school for the weekend. In addition, the principal had to pre-approve what we put up on the board. (No, we were not allowed to determine that for ourselves.) So nearly every Friday afternoon, I found myself standing outside the principal's office, hoping and praying that she would approve what I'd done so I could slap it on the bulletin board and then go home and enjoy my weekend. And of course, I was in good company. Most of the other teachers were right there with me.

While we waited to be seen by the principal, many of us would murmur complaints under our breath. "I went to college, and she's treating me like a child," we'd say. "Other principals allow their teachers to decide small matters like bulletin boards," we'd mutter.

It was a discouraging process, especially when the activity you'd done with your class and planned to display on the bulletin board was not approved. It only happened to me once, but I'll never forget it as long as I live.

It was my turn in the principal's office, and like every other week, I felt like a small child who'd been sent there for being naughty. I explained what I'd done with my class and asked if it was appropriate to go on the bulletin board in the hallway outside my classroom. She barely glanced at me while she said, "I think you can do a little better than that, Diane."

I was told that I needed to present her with something else by Monday afternoon. I left her office, feeling both angry and humiliated. The other teachers could tell by the look on my face that my activity was deemed "not good enough."

Over the weekend, I complained bitterly to my husband about the situation. "Maybe I'll just leave teaching," I said finally. "She's ruining it for me anyway."

My husband narrowed his eyes. "I don't think that's really what you want to do," he said. "But if you pray about it, and feel like God wants you to resign, I'll support it."

I shrugged. "I just know that I can't take much more of this."

But I took my husband's advice and began to pray about the situation. I didn't really want to leave teaching – I loved it. And I felt like God wanted me to continue. But I couldn't stand the bureaucracy I was seeing. And I didn't like being treated with disrespect. One morning in early May, I had made up my mind: I was going to resign. The stress was too much and I was getting out.

I opened my email and saw the following words from a friend: "I have told you these things, so that in me you may have peace. In this world you will have trouble. But take heart! I have overcome the world." (John16:33) And beneath the verse she'd written: "Get your chin up – it's dragging on the ground!"

Her words couldn't have come at a more opportune time. Yes, I was having trouble. Lots of it. But Jesus had overcome the world. I just had to overcome a principal on a power trip. Seemed like small potatoes compared to overcoming the whole world.

I realized that God didn't want me to quit teaching. That would be a cop-out, and I knew it. I needed to stay and overcome. But I needed His help to do it.

I got together with a few of the other teachers and we wrote up a list we called "Approved Bulletin Board Activities." Our thinking was this: if we could get the principal to agree to some pre-approved lessons, it would eliminate the Friday afternoon line of teachers in the office, as well as a lot of our stress. So the teachers could just choose a lesson from the list and know that it would be acceptable to the principal.

We took our list to the power-that-be and she actually agreed to it. She rolled her eyes and said, "Seeing all of you lined up outside my office every Friday was getting old anyway." And from then on, things really improved. The micromanaging seemed to ease up and she treated us with more respect.

If you're dealing with a stressful situation at school or at home, keep your chin up. Remember, Jesus overcame the world.

Prayer: Thank You, Lord, for Your Word. It includes so many promises and words of encouragement for us. Be with me as I try to overcome my own little part of the world. Amen.

Diane Stark

A Little Time-Out

Today you are officially on a Worry Break! There will be no worrying, no stressing out, and no stewing over anything. Give your problems to God and don't take them back!

Fake it 'Til Ya Make It

Above all, love each other deeply, because love covers over a multitude of sins.
1 Pater 4:8 (NIV)

Have you ever had a student who just rubbed you the wrong way? Drove you batty? Just stomped all over your very last nerve? I have. More than one, in fact. And while I'm not proud of it, I think sometimes, that poor child could sense that I didn't like him or her very much.

I know, that makes me a horrible teacher. But it also makes me human. No matter how much patience we have, most of us still have a few behaviors that really drive us nuts. The one that bugs me the most is whining. I have had students who seemed incapable of speaking in a normal tone of voice. These little darlings whined every time they opened their mouths.

And trust me, it wasn't so darling at the time.

One year, it seemed my entire class was comprised of whiners and complainers. Nearly every student, every single day, had a headache or a tummy ache or a hang nail. Someone had hurt their feelings, or looked at them funny, or crossed the invisible line between their desks. And they had to tell me about it. In their very best whiny voice.

It was a tough year for me. I felt crabby and short-tempered often. I had trouble bonding with these children because frankly, their whining got on my nerves.

One day, I was complaining to a dear friend about my roomful of whiners. And her advice was the some of the best I've ever been given. She said, "Fake it 'til ya make it." What she meant was that I needed to act as though I positively adored these children. I needed to give them my complete, undivided attention when they spoke. I needed to shower them with affection and praise when they did something well and to ignore the things they did that I didn't like. Oh, and I also needed to pray like crazy that God would fill my heart with a sincere love for these kids.

I took her advice. I acted lovingly toward these children, no matter how much they whined. And each time they annoyed me, I gave the unloving feelings to God. I asked Him to take my grumpy, not-so-Christian attitude and replace it with the feelings He has for those children. And little by little, it worked. After a few weeks of doing this, I hardly noticed the whining anymore. God helped me to truly love my students and as I Peter 4:8 says, "Love covers over a multitude of sins."

Even whining.

Prayer: Lord, help me to love my students today as You would love them. Help me to have a positive attitude toward each of them and act lovingly, no matter what.
Amen.

Diane Stark

A Little Time-Out

Is there something – or someone – you need to turn over to God? Is there something – or someone – you're worried about, stewing over, or otherwise feel bad about? If so, don't wait another minute. Give the situation to the one true God. He can help You, no matter what it is.

Help! I Need Somebody!

I can do everything through him who gives me strength.
Philippians 4:13 (NIV)

In my classroom is a bulletin board that reads, "Mrs. Stark's Helping Hands." This board is what I use to keep track of whose turn it is to do which job in our classroom. Each child's name is written on a laminated paper in the shape of a hand. On the board, our classroom jobs are listed. Things like: boy line leader, girl line leader, calendar helper, paper passer, lunch count helper, Pledge leader, and fish feeder. My students understand that if their paper hand is next to a certain job, that job is their responsibility for the week.

Every Monday, when my students enter our classroom, they go immediately to the Helper Board. If they have a job, they cheer. And if they don't have a job that week, they are disappointed and they can't wait to see if they'll have one the following week.

My students love helping me, but let's be honest. Sometimes their help isn't really all that helpful. I could pass out the papers much faster than my Paper Helper does it, and the lunch count takes a lot longer because I have help. And frequently, I have to go behind my little fish feeder and strain out the half-gallon of fish food they dumped in, or we risk having our poor goldfish suffocate.

Yes, kids love to help us, but oftentimes, their "help" causes us more work than it saves. We don't usually need their help, but it teaches kids some important lessons, makes them feel good about themselves, and they enjoy it. So it's worth the extra effort on our part.

And it reminds me of how God allows us to help Him do His work. He certainly doesn't need our help – He's the God of the Universe, so I think He can handle things without us lifting a finger! But like with our students, we learn some really great lessons when we do the Lord's work.

Some of the things that God asks us to do for Him may not be easy. They may be scary or difficult, or they may even seem downright impossible! But Philippians 4:13 says, "I can do everything through him who gives me strength." That means God will never ask us to do anything unless He's going to give us the strength to complete the task.

God doesn't need our help, but He allows us to take part in His plans. And better still, He promises to give us the strength to do what He asks.

Prayer: Lord, thank You for allowing me to help with Your plans. Help me to remember that You'll give me Your strength, and all I have to do is ask. Amen.

A Little Time-Out

Today look for ways to work smarter, not harder. Find another teacher and work out a way to help one another cut down on your work load. If you use the same materials, photocopy two sets and give one to her. And next week, she can do it for you. At my school, we share lesson plans as much as possible. Remember, work smarter, not harder.

The 180-Day Dash

Do you not know that in a race all the runners run, but only one gets the prize? Run in such a way as to get the prize. Everyone who competes in the games goes into strict training. They do it to get a crown that will not last; but we do it to get a crown that will last forever.
1 Corinthians 9:24-25 (NIV)

At my school, the best day of the entire year was always Field Day. Not only did we have the typical foot races and water balloon tosses, but our physical education teachers always planned some special surprise events that always drew a laugh. As a double bonus, our principal cooked the most delicious hamburgers on the grill. It was one of the few days that we teachers ate a school lunch without griping about it.

I always loved Field Day and I looked forward to it every year. But a few years ago, I had some special concerns about the event and I wasn't sure how it would work out. I had a child in my class who had cerebral palsy and I was worried about how she would handle all the physical activities. Hannah could walk, but she used crutches. She got around pretty well, but she couldn't go too fast or she would stumble.

At this school, the kindergarten students did not go to physical education classes, so our wonderful gym teacher was unaware of Hannah's condition. I wrote him a note, explaining the situation and requesting that she be placed in events where she would not be required to run. I assumed he received the note and would follow through.

Shame on me for not checking up. Somehow, the note never got to him and he put little Hannah in all of the events I was concerned she couldn't handle.

Including the three-legged race and the 50-yard dash. When Hannah's name was called to appear at the starting line for the three-legged race, I immediately went into panic mode. I pictured the worst happening: her falling down, getting hurt, and being embarrassed because she was different.

Again, shame on me. I didn't give Hannah – or her classmates - enough credit. What happened next still brings tears to my eyes. They paired Hannah with Jessica, another of my students. As the parent volunteer tied the girls' legs together, Jessica reached for one of Hannah's crutches and set it aside. "You only need one," she explained. "Because I will be your crutch on this side."

She wrapped her arm around Hannah's waist and said, "Lean on me and I won't let you fall."

While most of the kids counted one-two, one-two, alternating between their tied legs and free ones, the girls developed their own system. They moved their tied legs first, then Jessica waited until Hannah adjusted her crutch and then the girls moved their free legs together. They were slow and awkward, but somehow it was beautiful, watching one six-year-old be so careful and patient with another. Jessica wasn't worried about winning a ribbon. She was far more concerned about keeping her friend safe

While Hannah and Jessica didn't come in first, they still won the race in my eyes.

This story reminds me of how God wants us to go through our school year, as well as our lives. When Paul writes in 1 Corinthians 9:24 that we are to "run in such a way as to get the prize," I don't think he's referring to speed. He talking about living a life that pleases God, through the way we love other people.

So as you run the race of this school year, this 180-Day Dash, I would encourage you to do it like Jessica did. Run as to win the prize by being patient with those around you and careful with their feelings.

And when it gets difficult, remember Jessica's words to Hannah and picture God saying them to you.

"Lean on me and I won't let you fall."

Prayer: Lord, I pray that today You would remind me that I am running this race for You. Not for any prize in this lifetime, but for a crown that will last forever. Help me to run the race like You want me to. Amen.

Diane Stark

A Little Time-Out

This 180-Day Dash may not be over yet, but you still deserve a water break. Today, while grading papers and writing lesson plans, treat yourself to your favorite beverage. You've earned it!

Your Attention Please!

The Lord said, 'Go out and stand on the mountain in the presence of the Lord, for the Lord is about to pass by.'
Then a great and powerful wind tore the mountains apart and shattered the rocks before the Lord, but the Lord was not in the wind. After the wind there was an earthquake, but the Lord was not in the earthquake. After the earthquake came a fire, but the Lord was not in the fire. And after the fire came a gentle whisper.
1 Kings 19:11-12 (NIV)

A few years ago, I woke up on a Tuesday morning feeling as though my head might explode. And it felt like my throat already had. I felt horrible, but I had no fever, so I went to school.

But by the time I had arrived, I had completely lost my voice. When I whispered, the effort it required felt as though I were shouting. By lunch time, the school had gotten a substitute to replace me and I left to go to the doctor. (It turned out to be tonsillitis.) But as awful as I felt that day, I learned something really important.

When my students entered the classroom that morning, they saw the following message on the chalkboard: "Mrs. Stark has lost her voice so you will need to be extra quiet today." The kids read the message and then turned to me with concern in their eyes. I nodded and whispered, "I can't talk louder than this." I was worried that a few of my more challenging students might try to take advantage of this situation. Even I could understand the temptation. After all, no matter what they did, I couldn't yell at them today.

I was determined to keep as much to our normal schedule as possible, which meant reading a book aloud to the class as part of our morning activities. I grabbed the story I'd chosen for that day and sat in my rocking chair with the class gathered at my feet. I was sure that only the three or four children closest to me would be able to hear the book.

But my class surprised me. As I began to read in my loudest whisper voice, there were none of the usual noises, no wiggling or whispering, nothing. They were absolutely silent. You could have heard that proverbial pin drop in my room that day.

And the silence continued for the rest of the morning. The kids understood that if they were going to hear me, they had to be quiet. It was a wonderful, eye-opening experience. So much so, that I'm occasionally tempted to pretend to have laryngitis, just so my class will be quiet and cooperative.

I realized that day that there is power in a gentle whisper. I know teachers who, instead of trying to talk over their students, will whisper when their classroom gets too loud. It works. The kids are curious what we are going to say, so they get quiet so they can hear. It's a great way to calm everyone down, while gaining their attention at the same time.

Diane Stark

1 Kings 19:11-12 describes a time when the Lord appeared to Elijah. Elijah, in his human thinking, thought God would come to him in something powerful like a great wind, or an earthquake or a fire. But the Lord appeared to him through a gentle whisper. The King James Version calls it a "still, small voice."

Sometimes God gets our attention in ways that may seem small and insignificant to us. But in the hustle and bustle of our lives, we need to make sure we keep our hearts and ears open for His gentle whisper. That's one reason why having a daily devotional time is so important. It may be the only time all day in which we are quiet and focused enough to hear God's voice.

God has important things to tell us, but we have to be listening to hear Him.

Prayer: Help me, Lord, to be open to what You have to say to me today. Help me to remember that You are often in the little things in life. Amen

Diane Stark

A Little Time-Out

Try whispering to your class today. See if they aren't as quiet as church mice! It's always worked for me.

Call on Me

But in your hearts set apart Christ as Lord. Always be prepared to give an answer to everyone who asks you to give the reason for the hope that you have.
1 Peter 3:15 (NIV)

"I didn't get a turn," pouted Britney. "It's not fair. You called on everyone but me."

I glanced down at the math book from which we were working. "Honey, there are only eight problems on this page, and there are 22 students in the class. It's not possible for everyone to get a turn."

"It's still not fair," she muttered, her lower lip still poking out.

Many classrooms, especially lower elementary rooms, have this problem. Nearly every child feels that they "never get a turn" and they voice this complaint loudly and often.

Over the years, I've come up with a variety of methods to curb their complaints.

The easiest way is simply to keep track of how many times you've called on each child. If you're keeping a list, it's easy to keep things fair, which usually cuts down on the griping. (Although nothing I've found will eliminate it completely!)

I've used a classroom checklist and put a mark by each child's name as I've called on them. I've also written each child's name on a popsicle stick, put them in a cup, and as I remove each stick, I call on that child. The sticks don't go back in the cup until every student has had a turn. (Sounds fool-proof, but I have actually had kids think the stick with their name on it must have gotten lost!)

Some more creative ways include handing out tickets and the "price of admission" – or in this case, taking a turn – is the ticket. When everyone has turned in their ticket, everyone has gotten a turn.

Rarely, if ever, will kids think they've been treated completely fairly. They all want to be called on, often whether they know the answer or not. I think they usually know the answer when they raise their hand, but by the time their name is called, they have forgotten what they were going to say.

But as Christians, we are supposed to be prepared with an answer. We are called to remain hopeful in the Lord, and to tell anyone who asks us why we have hope. But I know many times in my own life, like my students, I have forgotten my answer by the time my name was called. (And way too often, I have forgotten to remain hopeful in the first place!)

But the apostle Peter writes, "But in your hearts set apart Christ as Lord. Always be prepared to give an answer to everyone who asks you to give the reason for the hope that you have." (1 Peter 3:15)

Most of the teachers I work with know that I am a Christian, and that means they watch me rather closely.

They look for evidence of my faith in my behavior. And while that's a lot of pressure, it also helps to keep me on track. I am an ambassador for the Lord, and I want to represent Him well.

So when it's my turn, I want to be ready with an answer. If someone calls on me and asks how I can be hopeful in this world, I will know what to say.
Will you?

Prayer: Lord, thank You that because of You, we can have hope in this life. We have hope because we know where we'll be spending eternity. Help me to point to You when someone asks me to give the reason for my hope. Amen.

A Little Time-Out

Make a list of reasons to be hopeful. Think of upcoming events that you've been looking forward to. Think back on memories of special times with family and friends. And most of all, remember that God loves you and sent His Son to die for all of us. Talk about a reason to be hopeful!

Diane Stark

Touching Lives

Nathan replied to the king, "Whatever you have in mind,
go ahead and do it, for the Lord is with you."
2 Samuel 7:3 (NIV)

When I was in first grade, I decided that I wanted to be a teacher when I grew up. I adored my first grade teacher, and I wanted to be just like her. In my eyes, she was no less amazing than Wonder Woman. (And I really liked Wonder Woman back then too.)

And that's why it always touches me when one of my students says they want to become a teacher when they grow up. Nearly every school year, one of my kindergarten students – usually a little girl - has said, "Mrs. Stark, when I grow up, I'm going to be a teacher, just like you." Those words warm my heart in a way that is almost indescribable. The words reaffirm that I'm doing a good job, that I'm doing what I was called to do. Those words tell me that I am representing my profession well. After all, nobody would want to grow up and be like me if I wasn't successful at what I was doing.

But one little girl's words touched me even more than the others. This little girl had a significant hearing loss and as a result, her speech was very difficult to understand. One day, she told me, "I would like to be a teacher when I grow up, but I don't think I can."

I knew why she would say that, but I asked anyway.

"Because," she said, "when I talk, people say "Huh? I don't understand you."

I put my arm around this sweet little thing and said, "Don't you let that – or anything else – stop you from doing what you want to do." Because I knew the girl's mother and I knew that they were believers, I added, "If God wants you to become a teacher, you'll become a teacher. No matter what."

She nodded and repeated my words. "No matter what."

Over my teaching career, I have worked with or heard about a number of teachers who face challenging situations. One of my dear friends is nearly completely blind, yet she teaches children with special needs. Her students see her challenges and they see her successes as well, and she is a powerful example to them. I know another teacher who is in a wheel chair due to multiple sclerosis. But she continues to teach because she loves it and knows she's making a difference.

Teaching is far more than a job. It's a calling. We're not there for the money; we're there for our students.

The Lord has a job for each one of us to complete while we are on this earth, and teaching has got to be one of the top jobs. We touch so many lives and we make such a difference. Every day, we have the opportunity to lift up and encourage children. We have the chance not only to teach them the required curriculum, but to care about them and make their lives better.

In the Bible, Nathan, a prophet, told King David, 'Whatever you have in mind, go ahead and do it, for the Lord is with you.' (2 Samuel 7:3) And God makes us that same promise. If you feel called to teach, the Lord will be with you as you fulfill that calling. He doesn't promise that it will always be easy, but He does promise to be with us. He gave us a job to do, and He'll give us everything we need to complete the assignment.

So the next time one of my students tells me that they want to be a teacher, I'm going to tell them to go for it. The rest of us would be honored to have them in our ranks.

Prayer: Lord, thank You for the chance to make a difference in some young people's lives. Help me to be a positive example to my students. Help them to see that I have You in my life. Amen.

Diane Stark

A Little Time-Out

Today take some time to look up one of your former teachers. Send them an encouraging note, telling them that you are a teacher today, in part, because of their example. I did this a few years ago, and it was one of the most rewarding things I've ever done. For both of us.

I Believe I Can Fly

Jesus looked at them and said, "With man this is impossible, but with God all things are possible."
Matthew 19:26 (NIV)

When I was student teaching, I taught in an inner-city school. This school was in a crime-ridden, drug-infested neighborhood in Indianapolis, Indiana. When I found out I was placed in a school like this, I was disappointed. I didn't want to teach in an inner-city school, but that was where my assignment was.

I learned quickly that kids are kids, no matter where they live. The students in this school certainly had more challenges than kids who live in more affluent areas, but their dreams were the same.

In this second grade class, only three children lived with both their mother and their father. Four students in the class had a parent who was incarcerated. Several more told me that one of their parents was addicted to drugs. All of these children were poor, and few of them believed they would be able to attend college someday.

On the last day of school, the kids watched the movie "Space Jam." While the credits were rolling, the song "I Believe I Can Fly" played. It seemed that every child knew the song's lyrics, and tears streamed down my cheeks as I listened to them sing.

"I believe I can fly," they sang. "I believe I can touch the sky."

"You guys really can fly, you know," I said when the song was over. "You can fly through life and make all of your dreams come true."

Several of them looked at me dubiously. Their eyes seemed to say, "But you know what kind of a home I come from. You know what I have to deal with. How can my dreams come true?"

But I said, "None of that matters. Work hard in school and stay out of trouble, and you can make your dreams come true. I don't care where you came from or who your parents are. You can succeed in this world if you make good choices."

Still, many of the kids shook their heads. They didn't believe that they could overcome their circumstances and become successful adults. They didn't think it was possible.

And in reality, the odds were stacked against them. Many of these kids had seen their older siblings get involved with gangs or drugs, or become pregnant at an early age. They didn't see many examples of success in their neighborhoods, so it was hard for them to believe they could achieve it themselves.

But we serve a God who doesn't worry about "the odds." He doesn't worry about what some say is unlikely or even impossible. In Matthew 19:26, Jesus makes an incredible promise. He says, "With man this is impossible, but with God all things are possible."

All things are possible. That means that those kids can fly through life and overcome their upbringing. And we can be amazing, effective teachers who show God's love to our students and fellow teachers.

Remember, with God, all things are possible.

Prayer: Lord, thank You for the many promises contained in Your Word. And help me to remember that when You say all things are possible, You really mean all things. Not most things – all things. Be with me as I go about my day. Amen.

A Little Time-Out

Write down three goals that seem impossible for you to achieve. They can be school-related or personal. And beginning today, pray about these goals and ask God to help you achieve them. Because remember, with Him, all things are possible.

Made in the
USA
Monee, IL